D1497919

The Terry Lectures
. .

THE STRUCTURE OF RELIGIOUS EXPERIENCE

THE TERRY LECTURES

*Volumes Published by the Yale University Press
on the Dwight Harrington Terry Foundation*

THE STRUCTURE OF
RELIGIOUS EXPERIENCE

BY

JOHN MACMURRAY

GROTE PROFESSOR OF PHILOSOPHY OF MIND AND LOGIC
UNIVERSITY OF LONDON, UNIVERSITY COLLEGE
LONDON, ENGLAND

40984

NEW HAVEN
YALE UNIVERSITY PRESS

Copyright 1936 by Yale University Press.

Printed in the United States of America.

———

First published, September, 1936
Second printing, July, 1941
Third printing, June, 1946

All rights reserved. This book may not be reproduced, in whole or in part, in any form (except by reviewers for the public press), without written permission from the publishers.

B L 53
·M 36

THE
DWIGHT HARRINGTON TERRY
FOUNDATION

LECTURES ON RELIGION IN THE LIGHT
OF SCIENCE AND PHILOSOPHY

THIS volume is based upon the sixteenth series of lectures delivered at Yale University on the Foundation
established by the late Dwight H. Terry of Plymouth, Con-
necticut, through his gift of $100,000 as an endowment fund
for the delivery and subsequent publication of "Lectures on
Religion in the Light of Science and Philosophy."

The deed of gift declares that "the object of this Foundation is not the promotion of scientific investigation and discovery, but rather the assimilation and interpretation of that
which has been or shall be hereafter discovered, and its ap-
plication to human welfare, especially by the building of the
truths of science and philosophy into the structure of a broad-
ened and purified religion. The founder believes that such a
religion will greatly stimulate intelligent effort for the improvement of human conditions and the advancement of the
race in strength and excellence of character. To this end it is
desired that lectures or a series of lectures be given by men
eminent in their respective departments, on ethics, the history
of civilization and religion, biblical research, all sciences and
branches of knowledge which have an important bearing on
the subject, all the great laws of nature, especially of evolution . . . also such interpretations of literature and sociol-
ogy as are in accord with the spirit of this Foundation, to the

end that the Christian spirit may be nurtured in the fullest light of the world's knowledge and that mankind may be helped to attain its highest possible welfare and happiness upon this earth . . .

"The lecturers shall be subject to no philosophical or religious test and no one who is an earnest seeker after truth shall be excluded because his views seem radical or destructive of existing beliefs. The founder realizes that the liberalism of one generation is often conservatism in the next, and that many an apostle of true liberty has suffered martyrdom at the hands of the orthodox. He therefore lays special emphasis on complete freedom of utterance, and would welcome expressions of conviction from sincere thinkers of differing standpoints even when these may run counter to the generally accepted views of the day. The founder stipulates only that the managers of the fund shall be satisfied that the lecturers are well qualified for their work and are in harmony with the cardinal principles of the Foundation, which are loyalty to the truth, lead where it will, and devotion to human welfare."

CONTENTS

INTRODUCTION

RELIGION stands at the crossroads. Throughout the world the parties of social progress are,
in general, either passively or actively anti-religious.
Organized religion, on the defensive, tends to range
itself, actively or passively, with the conservatives
and the reactionaries. But the tide of social evolution
cannot forever be dammed by the dykes of vested interest. The progressive forces are bound to win; and
it looks as though the bursting of the dykes would be
quick and catastrophic. If in that hour religion is
found still on the side of reaction, as it was in Russia,
it must suffer almost total eclipse. Its existing forms
will be doomed to destruction.

One of the main reasons for this fatal alignment
of religion with reaction is that the progressive attitude of mind is frankly empirical, while the religious
temper remains traditional and dogmatic. The empiricism which is at war with our religious traditionalism is bound up with science, and upon science the
progress of civilization increasingly depends. So our
house of life is divided against itself and cannot
stand. Our religious habit of mind, defending a tradition, pulls us backwards to the past, and fastens us
to forms of life which the march of development is
surely destroying. Our scientific empiricism draws
us into the future, toward the construction of new
habits and forms of life. Between the two tensions we

are paralyzed and can only stand helplessly watching the approach of catastrophe. In this dilemma of modern civilization, large numbers of people, with the Communists leading the vanguard, have sought release for the creative energy within them by cutting the religious cord that binds us to the past, and are marching, with banners flying, into the future, "without God and without hope in the world." They have pinned their faith to science, unaware that science cannot save the world, since it must serve and cannot lead. But there is another way out of the dilemma. If religion could abandon its traditional dogmatism and become itself empirically-minded, it could lead the progressive movement with science as its technical adviser. If this is impossible, then religion can no longer perform any positive function in a society which depends, even for its daily bread, upon the empirical temper of scientific research and technical inventiveness. Religion must either transform itself or fade away.

The chapters which follow are offered as a small contribution to this task of religious transformation. The argument is sustained by the belief, not merely that empiricism is compatible with religion, but that the only temper that is compatible with religious maturity is an empirical one. Traditionalism and dogmatism, I am convinced, are the marks of childishness and immaturity in every field of human experience. There is ample evidence, though it is generally overlooked, to justify the judgment that the empiricism of modern science is itself the product of Christianity. One has only to read the Christian Gospels to realize that it was for the realistic, empirical naturalism of his attitude that Jesus was hounded to death by the religious traditionalists of his day. A Christianity which has lost this empirical temper is a Christianity which has been falsified in the process of its history.

I have tried, therefore, to exhibit the essential structure of empirical religion and to explain the falsification by which it may become dogmatic and speculative. The hall mark of empiricism is its emphasis upon facts. It insists upon starting from facts and ending in facts; upon tying the inner activities of the mind tightly, at both ends, to the immediate realities of universal human experience. It demands that all theoretical processes should be consciously derived from an objective and unbiased determination of facts, and that at every point their results should be referred to the facts and checked by the facts. Accordingly, I have sought first to determine the field of fact, universally and directly recognizable, from which religious reflection properly arises. I have gone on to examine, in outline, the nature of the processes of religious reflection themselves; and I have concluded by discussing the nature of the reference to fact in terms of which religious assertions can be valid or invalid.

One of the main obstacles which has to be overcome before religion can recover its proper empiricism is

the current identification of empiricism with science.
The mature scientific attitude is necessarily empirical. It does not follow that all empiricism is necessarily scientific. Indeed, since religion and science are
not the same thing, a religious empiricism must differ from a scientific empiricism. I am concerned,
therefore, in the course of the discussion, to draw the
contrast between religious and scientific empiricism,
and to indicate the relation between them. This involves a reference to a third form of empiricism which
finds its appropriate expression in æsthetic activity.
Facts are meaningless until they are correlated and
organized and this is only possible through a process
of valuation. I have tried to show that the two antithetical principles of valuation which differentiate
art and science are one-sided limitations of the religious valuation-principle. If this be correct, it follows that the scientific and the æsthetic empiricism
are both partial empiricisms. Both presuppose yet
cannot deal with the group of facts which is the focus
of religious valuation, and which concerns the mutual
relationship of human beings and the sharing of a
common experience between them. The inclusion of
this group of facts, and its centrality in the religious
field, makes a religious empiricism more complete
than the limited empiricisms of science and art. The
religious empiricism provides the synthesis of the opposite and partial attitudes of art and science, and
this synthesis is necessary to the rationality of practical life. Cut loose from their unity in religion the

two partial empiricisms oppose one another and produce an antagonism in the field of social activity
which is destructive of order, freedom, and progress.
The salvation of the world is the task of religion. It
can be achieved neither by science nor by art. But a
religion which has deserted empiricism to defend
dogma and tradition has relinquished its task by
turning its back upon the facts of our common experience. The reward which it looks for in an imaginary
"other" world will, not unnaturally, prove an imaginary reward.

I

THE FIELD OF RELIGIOUS EXPERIENCE

HOWEVER far the intellect or the imagination may range beyond the limits of direct experience, it cannot cut itself loose from experience altogether. What is inferred must derive from what is not inferred but presented. What is imagined must be a transformation or a reorganization of what is directly given. This is as true for religion as it is for science. Science has its facts from which all its hypotheses, constructions, and laws are derived and to which they refer. These facts are ordinary data of universal human experience. The field of science is the whole body of common fact which it is the scientist's endeavor to understand. Religion, also, must have its ground and starting-point in facts of human experience. If it conceives another world than this, asserts its existence and so passes altogether beyond the limits of our experience in this world, it can only be because there are certain elements in our common experience of this world which constrain it to do so. Whatever else religion may be, or claim to be, it is at least a human activity, part of human behavior, one of the things that people do. It is no doubt a special kind of behavior. But it is made up of activities which are in no sense peculiar to religion. Men build a church precisely as they build a house.

It is only the function that is assigned to the two buildings that is different. The church could be used as a house, and the house could be used as a church. The ceremonial of religion is not essentially different from other ceremonial. It is only assigned a special meaning by those who take part in it. The effort of thought involved in the construction of a theology is not in itself distinguishable from the thinking that issues in a philosophy. In short, the special kind of behavior that we call religious is composed of the same elements as is behavior which is not religious. There is, perhaps, no element of human behavior which has not at one time or another, in one form or another, formed part of what we call religion. No doubt there is a special attitude of mind which transforms what would otherwise be non-religious behavior into behavior which is specifically religious. But an attitude of mind is an attitude to something. If it is to transform experience so that it acquires a special quality, there must be something in experience which can be so transformed, and which is not, apart from the religious attitude, religious. We have, therefore, to ask, "What is the field of religious experience?" What is it, that is to say, in human experience from which religion arises, and which the religious attitude of mind uses for the creation of religious behavior? What are the facts which have the same relation to religion that its data have to science?

It might be objected that if religion is illusory, as many people now insist, there will be no field in experience which forms the data of religion. But this is to misunderstand the question. The data of science are not themselves scientific, nor are the data of religion themselves religious. An illusory experience must arise from some facts which are not illusory, and to hold that religion is illusory is not to maintain that the data from which religion arises do not exist, but merely that religion distorts and misrepresents the data from which it starts. We are looking, that is to say, for a complex of elements in human experience which no one would deny, which are obvious and direct facts, and which provide the material which is transformed by the religious attitude into what we call religious experience. If an artist paints a portrait, the picture may be a good likeness or it may be almost totally unrecognizable. But in either case, the picture starts from the appearance of the real person as seen by the artist or by anyone else. The scientist's account of a bar of copper certainly transforms it out of all recognition, much more than the worst portrait that was ever painted. But in every case these activities of transformation must start from something which is normal fact in human experience. The scientist, the artist, and the religious man—all must start from a range of experience which is common to all men everywhere; even though it is true, perhaps, that only a few have the capacities which are necessary to produce the transformation that creates religion or art or science.

What, then, is the field of religious experience?

What are the normal and universal facts of human experience out of which religion, as a special kind of human behavior, arises? This is the question to which we have to find an answer. It is impossible to give any account of religion without answering this question, though it is possible to answer it without knowing that we have done so. Whenever anyone talks about religion, he assumes that there is a field of religion, a field of real, direct experience out of which religious phenomena emerge, and the way he interprets religion will reveal the kind of facts which he has in mind. If someone maintains that religion is a product of fear, he implies that the field of religion is the field of terrifying facts in human experience. If a psychologist maintains that the idea of God is an unconscious projection of the father, he defines the field of religion as the universal experience that we all have as children in relation to our parents. In all cases the field is a field of normal, universal, and uninterpreted human experience. If, however, we are to give a *true* account of religion, it is of primary importance that we should answer this question about its empirical field correctly. If we omitted this we should be acting like biologists who should offer an account of the behavior of an organism without taking the trouble to discover the stimulus to which it is a response.

Now, a great deal of our modern study of religion is in this condition. It attempts to give an account of the response without any reference to the stimulus. Any theory of religion which confines itself to the phenomena of religious practice or religious belief, any theory for which the varying forms of religious behavior are the data on which its account of the nature of religion is to be based, cannot provide an understanding of religion because it fails to relate the specific forms of religious behavior to the field of ordinary experience in which they arise. To an observer, for example, who had no knowledge of religion whatever, prayer would appear simply as a man talking to somebody who wasn't there. Such an observation would be inexplicable if no attention were paid to the normal experience of one man talking to another who is there. The religious man could only explain his behavior to the observer by saying that he was speaking to God, and that in turn by reference to the ordinary use of speech between men.

The first difficulty which meets us when we try to answer our question is that it seems impossible to distinguish any special set of facts which form the field of religion. All the facts of experience seem to be data for the religious consciousness. We shall see this clearly if we try to distinguish the field of religion from the field of science. There is no fact of experience which the scientist will not claim as part of his data. Science takes the whole world of experience and leaves nothing over for religion. But equally, religion claims the whole world of experience for itself. The artist does likewise. We are driven, therefore, to suppose that the difference between them must lie not in their fields but in the attitudes of mind in which

they deal with the same field. The facts are there. But
the religious man brings a different attitude of mind
to bear upon them from the scientist or the artist.
Starting from the same facts, religion and art and
science move in different directions because they deal
with the facts differently. The religious man comes to
worship, the artist to admire, the scientist to observe.
But they all come to the same world of common fact.
Before accepting the truth that lies in this remark,
there are two qualifications which we must make. In
the first place, science, art, and religion are not three
sets of people. The same person may be at once religious, artistic, and scientific. The three attitudes of
mind which we have distinguished can be combined in
one and the same mind. We ought to restate the distinction by saying that if we approach the facts in
an attitude of worship we shall find that we are in the
field of religion, whereas if we approach the same
facts in the attitude of mere observers, we shall find
ourselves in the field of science. The second qualification is this. The scientist, though he claims all the
facts as his field, finds that certain groups or aspects
of the facts lend themselves much more readily to his
manner of approach than others. The artist and the
religious man find themselves at home with quite another group of facts or another aspect of the field.
Certain things are easier to observe and analyze than
others. Certain things are easier to admire and contemplate with satisfaction than others, and certain
facts are much more easily reverenced. Thus, though

when we generalize we have to say that the field is one
and the same for science, art, and religion, when we
come down to earth and begin to grapple with the
field in all its complexity we find that in practice
there are three fields which overlap to a considerable
extent but which have distinct centers. It is as if the
same field of general experience became organized in
three different ways round three different centers of
interest. The velocity with which a body falls to the
earth lies very near the center of interest for science.
But for religion it lies somewhere near the circum-
ference. In practice, therefore, the scientist will find
himself continually preoccupied with one set of facts
and the religious man with another, because it is in
terms of the selection defined by his attitude of mind
that he must deal with all the facts. In this sense, science, art, and religion, though they are concerned in
an abstract sense with the whole of experience, will
actually start from different fields, and seek from
their different centers to bring an ever enlarging
range of experience into relation with their own starting-point. When we remember this our question about
the field of religion becomes manageable. It means,
"What are the facts and aspects of common human
experience to which we turn, and in which our interest centers, when we approach the world in a religious frame of mind?"

These considerations reveal a factor of real importance for our inquiry. The three attitudes of mind in
which we approach the world of common experience

have the effect of selecting parts of it for special attention. Now, selection is valuation, and we cannot select one thing from among a number of others without assigning it a higher value than the others, at least in respect of our immediate purpose. If an attitude of mind toward the whole field of experience selects a particular part of the field as central, it organizes experience thereby in terms of a scale of relative values. What it makes central becomes, for that very reason, the most important fact, and the one in terms of which all the others gain or lose importance. The scientific attitude selects as central those facts of experience which are most clearly and accurately observable, that is to say, what can be measured and counted. These become for it the most important facts in the world, while the others become less important and lie further from the center. This enables us to understand the tendency of a scientific age to think that the material aspects of experience are its *real* aspects. Science is materialistic, not because the real is material, but because its interests are scientific. It selects the measurable aspect as the most important, because it is the aspect with which it can deal. In this it is following the natural and inevitable anthropomorphism of all human behavior. Its principle is the shoemaker's principle that there's nothing like leather.

The fact that these attitudes of mind are bound up with valuation provides us with a clue. Valuation is primarily a feature of practical activity. It is con-

cerned originally with the necessity of choosing between possible activities. The attitudes which lie
behind religion and art and science are reflective attitudes, and must themselves be derived from the common field of practical experience. Now, in ordinary
life we value some things for themselves, while we
value others not for themselves but for the use that
we can make of them. Philosophers, therefore, have
distinguished between utility value and intrinsic
value. The distinction is too well known to require
elaboration. Anything that we use has a utility value
for us in the act of using it. On the other hand anything that has an intrinsic value is important to us by
being what it is. In action its importance is not that
we use it, not that it serves our purpose, but simply
that it is there for us. In action we seek to possess it
or to make it our own. Now, if we turn from action
to reflection, these two types of value determine two
different attitudes of mind. If our reflection selects in
terms of utility value, the kind of knowledge we seek
is very different from the kind of knowledge we seek
if our reflection is grounded in intrinsic value. In the
first case, we shall find ourselves investigating things
in order to find out what are the characteristics that
make them useful or useable. Two consequences follow. We shall be interested in the causal properties of
things and we shall endeavor to secure general knowledge. For the causal properties of anything are precisely the characters which make it useable, and our
interest in it is only a general interest. I mean by this

that if our only interest in a thing lies in the possibility of using it for a purpose, what we shall want to know about it is not what distinguishes it from other individuals of the same kind but what it has in common with them. Whereas, if its value to us is intrinsic, it is precisely its unique individuality that interests us. Now, knowledge of causal properties and general characteristics is precisely the kind of knowledge which we seek and gain in science. We are driven, therefore, to the conclusion that the attitude of mind which determines the selection and organization of the field of science is defined by a valuation of experience in terms of utility. The most general characteristics of the world become central. What the data have in common takes precedence of their differences. Causal properties become all-important. The facts of science are the ordinary data of experience selected in their material aspects, since it is their material characteristics that make things useable and give them their utility value.

This conclusion is strengthened if we compare it with the result of reflecting in terms of intrinsic value. Let us take a very simple example. Suppose that I have seen displayed for sale a piece of carved jade which I thought so beautiful that I wished to possess it; but that its price was more than I could afford. That valuation may determine activity. I may set to work to earn or to save sufficient money to buy it, and this will, of course, involve a modification of my activity. But while I am working to provide the

means for buying it, or after I have made it my own,
there will arise an activity of reflection which is concerned with the object. This reflection will not be of
the scientific type at all, as it would be if the thing I
wanted was for use. It will be an effort to fill my
mind with the object; to remember or to realize more
fully the unique qualities which make me single it out
as valuable in itself. Indeed, my possessing it in the
economic sense is only a preliminary to my desire to
possess it in another and much more important sense.
I want to have it there so that I can look at it again
and again, and so make it my own by imprinting its
image again and again upon my mind; reviving and
deepening the impression that it first made upon me.
Because the value that it has for me is intrinsic, in
reflection my attitude toward it is contemplative and
emotional, not analytic and intellectual. The knowledge of it that I seek is not a knowledge of its properties and general characteristics, but simply an increasing familiarity with itself, which issues in a
deepening and better grounded admiration. Now
these are precisely the defining characteristics of the
artistic attitude. If this attitude is brought to bear
upon the whole field of common experience it will define and organize it in a very different way from the
scientific attitude. What will now become central is
not what can be most easily utilized but what can be
most joyfully contemplated and admired. Beauty is
the name we give to that which makes anything good
to contemplate in its concrete individuality. The ar-

tistic attitude, therefore, organizes the data of experience in terms of their beauty. The more beautiful anything is the more near it lies to the center of interest. This must result in a very different selection and ordering of experience, one indeed which is the antithesis of the order which the scientific attitude creates. For the more generally useful a thing is, the less individuality it possesses. The more unique anything is—the more it possesses an intrinsic value of its own—the less generally useful it is apt to be for practical purposes. Money is one of the most useful things in civilized life, and therefore one dollar is as good as another. But if by chance I came to prize as a keepsake a dollar that was given me on a memorable occasion by a famous statesman, it would cease to have any utility value for me by acquiring intrinsic value. I could no longer spend it without doing violence to my sentiment.

We have now distinguished two attitudes of mind in which we can approach the world of common experience. We might call them the practical attitude and the contemplative attitude. If instead I have used the terms scientific and artistic to describe them, it is simply to call attention to the fact that they are the two attitudes which define the field of science and the field of art respectively by the different valuation which they impose upon experience to organize it. The scientific attitude, approaching all the data of experience with the feeling that they are things for use, sees the world as consisting of different stuffs

that can be used for different purposes. It finds
water, fire, air, earth, wood, stone, metal. On further
reflection these obvious stuffs dissolve into others less
obvious. The world becomes oxygen, hydrogen, chlo-
rine, aluminium, copper, sulphur, and so on, together
with the forces which move these elements—combin-
ing them and separating them—light, heat, electric-
ity, magnetism, gravitation. On further reflection
still, these too split up into masses of indistinguish-
able units, electrons and protons, or perhaps merely
a crisscross of ripples kept going and coming by
strains and stresses in a primordial matrix so indis-
tinguishable that it can be identified with the empti-
ness of mere Space-time.

What is noticeable in the progression of this scientific picture is that it moves always away from individuality toward an undistinguishable commonness.
The artistic attitude, in reflection, moves in the
opposite direction toward individuality and unique-
ness. Bringing to experience the desire to contemplate and admire, it sees the world as a collection of
unique and interesting objects. The more definite and
stable they are, the more possible it is to single them
out for contemplation. In reflection it passes from the
concentration upon easy and superficial beauty to
deeper and more difficult forms, from the obvious
beauty which is evanescent and fleeting to beauties
that are enduring and eternal. What distresses it
most is the changeableness of the things of experience. Individuality is everywhere subject to fading

and dissolution. Nothing keeps its beauty long. So
the artist seeks, as we say, to immortalize what is in
experience evanescent. He seeks to make what is passing a possession forever; to confer on the data of
common observation an individuality which can defy
time; to prevent what is unique from being wholly
reabsorbed into the common dust from which it arose.
The same contrast can be observed in the effect of science and art upon human activities. The effect of science is to emphasize and accelerate the processes of
change. The way in which science transforms not
merely social life but the face of the earth itself is a
commonplace among us. The effect of art upon us is
the opposite. It leads to the effort to maintain and
preserve against the ravages of time things which
have for us an intrinsic value. Not merely ancient
works of art but ancient ceremonial, ancient buildings are carefully guarded and preserved; and even
corners of the world which have struck man by their
natural beauty, like the Yosemite Valley, are carefully and expensively preserved against the scientific
attitude which would dissolve their beauty in an effort to exploit them for practical purposes.

What, then, is the field of religion? Is there a
third, distinct form of valuation imposed upon common experience by the religious attitude? If there is,
what does it select, and how does it organize experience? It would seem at first sight that there is no
room for another type of valuation. If values are
either utility values or intrinsic values, things can be

valued as ends in themselves or as means to other ends. What room is there for a third type of value which would be neither the one nor the other?

Now, though it might seem at first sight that there could be no room for another form of valuation, a little reflection will convince us that there must be. We have seen that the artistic and the scientific attitudes are antithetical and tend to achieve opposite results both in reflection and in action. But both attitudes are common to all of us. Both forms of valuation are attitudes of one and the same person. Though at points we find an antagonism between the two in our own minds, we do not normally feel that there is any incompatibility between them. There are very many things that we value both for their utility and for themselves. Indeed, we often look upon the failure to combine these two attitudes as a mark of barbarism. Tools have utility value primarily. They are for use. Yet a good craftsman grows to love the tools which he uses so that they acquire for him an intrinsic value, and he cares for them beyond the point which is necessary from a purely utilitarian point of view. It is an instinct with man even from the most primitive times to seek to combine utility and beauty. If one and the same mind, then, can adopt either of these attitudes; if men can seek for the combination of utility and intrinsic value in the things they produce or acquire, then there must be an attitude of mind which combines the two antithetical attitudes. For if there were not, human personality would be

split in two and radically at war with itself. It is quite
obviously characteristic of religion that it does seek
this combination. Some forms of religion stress the
utilitarian attitude; others the æsthetic. Religion has
always been associated with the need that men have
felt for help and assistance, and part of the religious
attitude has always looked upon religion as a practical means of achieving its ends. But it is equally certain that religion has always looked upon its activities as important in themselves, imbued with an
intrinsic value of their own. Primitive religious ceremonial is both an expression of the sense of beauty
and a means of securing the welfare of the tribe. The
Lord who is to be worshiped in the beauty of holiness
is also a very present help in time of trouble. Christianity has always insisted on the absolute intrinsic
value of the individual. But it has also equally insisted that his value lies in doing the will of God and
making himself the instrument of a divine purpose.
Nor have Christians felt that there was any contradiction in this paradox. Instances of this combination
in religion of the practical and the contemplative attitudes can be multiplied at will. We may therefore
conclude, not merely that there must be an attitude
of mind which synthesizes the two opposites, but that
the activities of religion are rooted in it, and are at
least one of the forms of its expression.

In describing the two attitudes which determine the
scientific and the artistic field we assumed that the
field of common experience was just there; standing

over against us, as it were; waiting for us to impose
our valuation upon it. It was there for our use or for
our pleasure. On the other hand, it appeared as a
matter of accident whether we adopted one attitude
or the other. We had forgotten that we ourselves are
part of the field of common experience. For each of
us all the rest of us are data. Our situation is not
completely expressed by saying, "Here is the world;
how shall we value it?" It is also, "Here we are; what
value have we in the world? How are we to value
ourselves? And how are we to value one another?"
Against the question, "What are we to make of the
world?" we must set the question, "What is the world
to make of us?" It is only when we take both these
sides of experience together that we grasp the field of
common experience as a whole. We and our attitudes
of mind are part of the world. And in this complete
field of experience it is we who are partial, tempo-
rary, and dependent. The attitude of mind in which
we realize this, in which we set ourselves in the world
as dependent creatures of it, is a very different attitude of mind from the other two that we have discussed; and the valuation which it imposes, the organization of the data which it necessitates, are very
different. It is this attitude which is the attitude of
religion.

If this, then, is the religious attitude of which we
were in search, what is the field of common experience which it defines as the field of religion? In particular, what are the central data which become the

focus of importance and round which, in relation to which, all the others are organized?

We must notice first that the religious attitude actually enlarges the scope of the field. When we agreed that the field of science was the whole range of common experience, we were in fact leaving ourselves out. We were in fact setting the world of common experience over against ourselves, and to that extent it was less than the whole of the data. The field of religion is therefore wider and more complete than the field of science or of art. It may be objected that science in psychology does take us and our activities in as parts of the field of science. In a sense this is true. But it is also true that we appear as data in the field of psychological science only partially. In the field of religion, each of us appears twice, both as the source of valuation and as the object of valuation. In psychology I appear as the object that is described, analyzed, and explained; and in activity which is based upon scientific psychology, I appear as the patient who is treated or manipulated by psychological devices, such as advertisement and propaganda. But I do not appear as that which describes and analyzes, nor as that which treats me or manipulates me. But in religion I appear in both these aspects and in both at once. When the Psalmist says, "What is Man that Thou art mindful of him, or the Son of Man that Thou visitest him?" or when he cries, "We are as the grass of the field which today is and tomorrow is cast into the oven"; when the Prophet exclaims, "Thou

art God and there is none else," the essential fact
about these statements is that though they assert the
nothingness of man, it is man who asserts them. It is
characteristic of the religious valuation that it as-
signs a very high value to the human judgment that
sets a very low value on its own activities, including
its judgments. This is a paradox, but it is also a description of the data of ordinary human experience.

This simple fact that we are able and indeed com-
pelled to pass judgment upon ourselves lies very near
the center of the religious field. As pronouncing
judgment we are outside the field of experience; but
as judged we are inside it. In other words, we are
both transcendent of experience and immanent in it.
This union of transcendence and immanence is, then,
the full fact about human personality. It is an empirical fact and a natural fact. We are accustomed
to find it applied in theology to God, and it is usually
assumed to be a peculiar and distinguishing attribute
of Deity. We see now that this is a mistake. The union of immanence and transcendence is a peculiar and
defining characteristic of all personality, human or
divine; but it is primarily a natural, empirical fact
of common human experience. Religious reflection
applies it to God as a defining characteristic of universal personality because it finds it in experience as
a given fact of all finite personal experience.

But this capacity for self-judgment is not quite
primary. It involves an effort of reflection. There is a
more primitive character of common experience of

which it is the first derivative, of which, indeed, it is only an aspect. The primary fact is that part of the world of common experience for each of us is the rest of us. We are forced to value one another, and the valuation is reciprocal. It is this point to which I must draw special attention because it is the organizing center of the field of religion. When I deal with things in the world which are not human beings, I can treat them as subject to any valuation which I like to impose. I can either use them or admire them. But, if the objects I have to deal with are other people, this is impossible, for a very simple reason. The attitude which I take up sets a value on them, no doubt; but while I am valuing them they are valuing me. While I ask myself what I am to make of them, how I am to treat them, they are asking themselves what they are to make of me, and how they will treat me. It is this that makes the relations between ourselves and other people completely different from our relations with anything else in the world. It sets the central problem of human life, and it is a religious problem. It is this central fact to which Jesus drew attention when he said, "Judge not, that ye be not judged; for with what judgment ye judge, ye shall be judged, and with what measure ye mete it shall be measured to you again." It is the fact that all personal relationships are mutual and reciprocal in their very nature.

The full significance of this can only be grasped if we see it in terms of action, not of thought and re-

flection. It is in action that we have to relate ourselves to the things in the world. It is the necessity of
living that forces us to impose our valuation on
things. Religion, the religious attitude, and the religious valuation, with the conception of the world
which it organizes, are forced upon us by the necessity of entering into relation with other people if we
are to live at all. We must, therefore, impose our
valuation upon people, but in doing so we force them
equally to impose their valuation upon us. This is, in
fact, what we all do in life, whether we reflect about it
or not. If, then, I adopt an attitude to another person that gives him for me a utility value merely, I
say to him in effect, "You are for my use." The only
possible reply that he can make is a flat denial, and if
we are to work together on these terms at all, he will
have to assert in turn that I am for his use, and each
of us will be trying to use the other for his own ends.

The artistic attitude equally fails to establish satisfactory relations between people. The valuation it imposes would be expressed if I said to another person,
"You have an intrinsic value for me. You are for my
enjoyment." The kind of action to which this valuation would give rise would be that I should seek to
possess the other person as an object of permanent
value to myself, not for use but for enjoyment. If I
could succeed I should be the owner of a priceless
treasure. The other person would have value in himself for me. But this would be incompatible with his
having a value in himself for himself. Along those

lines personal relationships could only become reciprocal by establishing a permanent mutual admiration
society, in which each of the members sought to keep
hold of the others for the emotional satisfaction of
watching them with admiration.

What is required in our relations with one another,
if we are to recognize in practice the essential reciprocity of the relationship, is an attitude which some-
how contains both of the other two attitudes while
transcending them both. Coöperation in activity does
require that I should think of other people as having
a utility value, but in such a way that I also have a
utility value. I cannot do this if their utility value is
imposed by me. For then I should be master and they
would be my servants. If we are all to have a utility value for one another, it must be imposed by all
of us, or by none of us. Yet all human coöperation is
necessarily on a basis of mutual service, which makes
each of us a servant. Obviously this implies that each
of us values all the others for themselves. Why else
should I set aside my own claim to use them in my
service in order to serve *them*. But this involves a reference from the scientific to the artistic attitude, from
a recognition of utility value to a recognition of intrinsic value. By itself the artistic attitude would
prevent me from allowing them to serve me, and
would so make coöperation impossible. If, then, we
are to enter into relations with one another, it has to
be in terms of an attitude to one another which is able
to unite these two attitudes, and so to combine utility

value and intrinsic value. This attitude is a religious attitude, and it is best expressed in terms such as fellowship or communion. We have to enter into fellowship with one another and so to create community.

We have now answered our question and defined the field of religious experience. The field of religion is the whole field of common experience organized in relation to the central fact of personal relationship. It is the personal data which are central, and form the focus of attention. Everything else is seen, from the religious point of view, in its relation to personality. The personal is the fact of central importance. All other facts are valued in relation to this central value. To put it in simpler if less exact language, the field of religion is the field of personal relations, and the datum from which religious reflection starts is the reciprocity or mutuality of these. Its problem is the problem of communion or community. Religion is about fellowship and community, which are facts of direct, universal human experience. This is the main point which we had to determine. But before passing on to consider the self in religious activity we should notice that this religious field is more ultimate than either the field of art or the field of science. For it includes the data of common experience which are left out by art and science, and the attitude which determines and orders it contains in itself and combines the two attitudes which in isolation from one another determine the fields of science and of art respectively.

II

THE SELF IN RELIGIOUS REFLECTION

THE complication of the argument in the last chapter tends a little to obscure the fundamental simplicity of its conclusion. The position which it establishes can be stated in a few words. The field of religion is the field of personal experience. The center of this field is the experience we have of other persons in relation to ourselves. In all our relations with one another we are in the field of religion; and since there is nothing in the whole range of our experience which may not be seen and valued in its bearings upon our relations with one another, there is nothing at all which does not belong, directly or indirectly, to the field of religion. It is a simple commonplace that the lives of human beings are interdependent. Other people bring us into the world and other people bury us when we die, and all our life through we are dependent in a thousand ways upon other people. That is the simple fact; and it means that the structure of human experience, dependent as it is for its very existence upon the mutual relations of persons, is religious in its texture. It is this primary fact about us that gives rise to religion, and since this is a universal fact about human life, belonging to its very nature, it follows that religion is an inseparable component of human life and always must be. To say

that religion belongs to the early stages of human life
and is destined to be superseded as human development goes on is to talk foolishness. That could only
be true if progress reached the point when we were
all hatched out by the sun on desert islands and lived
and died without knowing that there was anyone else
in the world but our solitary selves. A person who has
no religion, or a society which has repudiated religion, has merely forgotten that humanity exists only
in the relation of human beings to one another.

We are concerned now to discuss the self in its religious activity. In doing this we are trying to discover how religion, as a specific human activity, arises
out of the primary facts of human relatedness. This
depends primarily upon the attitude of mind in which
the self deals with its experience. It is a fact that we
are interdependent. But we are often unconscious of
this fact. We take it for granted and concentrate our
attention upon other aspects of our experience, so
that they fill the field of our consciousness. The religious attitude, therefore, is that attitude of mind
for which our relations to other people are central.
The religious life is the life which is dominated by
this belief in the centrality of personal relations. Any
attitude of mind, as we have seen, imposes an order of
valuation upon the world of its experience. The religious attitude sets the relationship of the self to other
selves as the center of valuation and values everything else in relation to this. For such an attitude
the main business of life consists in understanding,

appreciating, and creating the full reality of personal relationship. The task of religion is the realization of fellowship. The religious activity of the self is its effort to enter into communion with the Other.

Our interest in the reflective activities is very apt to blind us to the fact that they are never primary. We are apt to think that scientific experience is the experience of a set of experts who have made it their business to develop scientific knowledge. But scientific experience is primarily the universal experience that we all have of manipulating material things. It is our experience in the scientific field, whether we are scientists or not. Science is simply the specialized effort of a few people to concentrate upon achieving the knowledge of things which enables everybody to manipulate and use them more effectively. Religion, in the sense in which we usually refer to it, is the reflective aspect of a universal human experience, the experience of living in relation to one another. But there is this difference between religion and science, that the separation of the reflective aspect of religious activity from the primary life of religious experience is not possible, while in the scientific field it is. If it is a question of building a house, an architect can think out to the last detail how the house shall be built and then get other people to do the building. A division of labor between the person who does the thinking and the person who does the practical work is possible. The former can act through agents. But no one can enter into fellowship with another person through

agents. If I am concerned to improve my relations
with other people, no doubt thought and meditation
and other forms of reflective activity can help a great
deal. But the results of these cannot be achieved by
getting somebody else to act upon them. Only my own
behavior is of any avail. In the field of personal relations, which is the field of religion, we cannot act
through agents.

Consider the simplest case of all, that of the relations of a husband and wife. For each of the two the
satisfactoriness of their mutual relation is fundamental to everything else in their individual lives. They
share a common life, and that common life consists of
mutual coöperation in a routine of daily activity
which is much more than a mere coöperation, since it
is itself a fellowship in life. That is its primary aspect
as the universal practical experience of lived and living relationship. But it produces also, within itself,
as it were, a *reflective* life of fellowship, when their
relationship to one another becomes the focus of attention for them. When they turn from the practical
coöperation in a common life, after the day's work is
done, to enjoy one another's company, their life of
fellowship becomes for the time an end in itself. It is
possible in this way to distinguish within their common life two aspects, one in which their fellowship is
merely a fact which determines the structure of a
common life in which they coöperate for all sorts of
purposes which they have in common, and another in
which enjoying, developing, and deepening the fel-

lowship has itself become the purpose which governs
their mutual activities. These two aspects are so inseparably interwoven that they cannot really be separated.

We have been assuming that the fellowship between
the two was completely satisfactory in both its aspects. But the harmony of the mutual relationship
is always liable to be broken. If for any reason the
relations between husband and wife become strained,
something must be done about it or the common
life will be wrecked. In this situation communion is
broken and what is required is reconciliation. The
first effect of this appearance of enmity between two
persons who are bound together in a common life is
paradoxical. They are isolated from one another in
their unity. The unity remains unbroken, because
they do and must share a common life. The unity is
broken because in consciousness they are in opposition to one another at every point within the common
life. They love one another and yet they hate one another. And the hatred falls within the unity of love. If
it did not the unity would simply be broken and the
common life would cease to exist and could not be restored. We might almost go so far as to say that when
two lovers quarrel they hate one another because they
love one another. This isolation of each within the
unity that binds them together is a clash between two
wills which are bound to coöperate. Its effect is to
throw each of the two people back upon themselves.
If the harmony is to be restored, it must be upon the

initiative of one or the other acting independently. And that can only be if one or the other changes his mind. A change of heart, or a change of mind, is the condition of a reconciliation. There is here another aspect of reflection in the life of fellowship. When husband and wife are in harmony, the reflective life of fellowship is an enjoyment of one another's company. But if the harmony is broken between them, each is necessarily driven into consciousness of his relation to the other; reflection, of which the fellowship is the focus, is forced upon them. But in this case it is for each a solitary reflection, not a mutual one, and the act which will restore the fellowship must be a solitary act, a gesture from one or the other which will break the tension. Since each feels injured by the other, that gesture, whatever form it may take, is a gesture of forgiveness, or a plea for forgiveness; in most cases it will be both at once. As a plea for forgiveness it is an acceptance of individual responsibility for the broken harmony and so a confession of guilt. Mutual forgiveness secures a reconciliation which breaks down the isolation in which each was shut away from the other, and so restores the unity that was there all the time but was interrupted in consciousness. In such a reconciliation, if it is real and not a compromise, another paradox appears which is of considerable importance for metaphysics as well as for religion. It is the fact that the estrangement that has been overcome, though it is for both parties a matter of regret, also results in a strengthening and deepening of the unity between them. The estrangement is not merely forgiven and forgotten. It is utilized for the development of the unity which it interrupts. It is, perhaps, an essential component of any such unity, if it is to be more than superficial.

In examining such a simple example of human relationship we have been considering the self in its primary religious activity. You will notice that although the analysis has been quite superficial and the description quite simple and direct, yet already the words and ideas which have emerged are just those with which we are familiar in religion. To describe the everyday experience of two people sharing a common life we have had to use such words as fellowship, communion, enmity, estrangement, guilt, forgiveness, reconciliation. These terms, therefore, in their religious usage are quite obviously derived from the universal human experience of the life of personal relationship. Indeed, it is not merely the terms or the ideas that are so derived. All the varied forms in which religion has expressed itself are to be found directly in the forms of such simple and commonplace human relations; and most of the paradoxes which have puzzled the minds of theologians and philosophers, and which have seemed to many people to show that religion is a fantastic tissue of irrational conceptions, are merely the descriptions of facts which are so common and universal in our daily experience that we hardly notice them. Religion, in fact, is simply the universalization in reflection of this central factor in human experience. The universalizing of particular experience is the defining characteristic of reason, so that we can understand why religion is the primary expression of reason in human life. It is primary not merely in the sense that it is the earliest in time, but in the sense that the experience which it universalizes is the primary experience of all men and the functional center of all human life.

Before describing the activity of the self which creates religion by universalizing the direct experience of mutual relationship, I should like to refer briefly to two other features of the primary experience itself. The first concerns the history of the individual, the other the history of human society. The individual is born into a family. He is the creation of a personal relationship. His earliest experience, which lays the foundation of all his future behavior, is an experience of complete and helpless dependence on other people for the supply of all his needs. In this earliest experience the unity is complete though one-sided. But that primitive unity of dependence cannot continue. It is necessarily broken in a way that throws the child back on himself and isolates him, so that he becomes conscious of himself as a separate individual. It is then that he begins, in the cunning way that children have, to discover means for protecting himself against the unkindness of people who will not always do what he wants or give him what he demands. He discovers means of placating the all-powerful beings on whom he is dependent

when they are offended, and of coaxing and whee-
dling them into compliance with his wishes. The experience of estrangement within the relationship, with
its discovery of anger and hatred for the people he
loves, is essential to the creating of his individuality.
Through it he learns to have a will of his own, which
opposes and is opposed by wills which are stronger
than his. Yet this creation of individuality is possible
only within the fellowship which binds him to those
whom he both loves and hates. In the long run, when
he is grown to maturity, the real crisis comes. The relation of dependence has to be broken. He is forced
into an isolation of his own individuality more complete than he has ever known, and he is faced with
the necessity of creating for himself a new relationship which is no longer one of dependence but one of
equality.

Modern psychologists have been very much im-
pressed by the obvious analogy between religious behavior and the behavior of children in early life in
relation to their parents. God is seen by the psycho-
analysts as the projection of the father, and the
adult's attitude to God as the imaginary projection
of his childish attitudes to his father which have per-
sisted, as suppressed and unresolved conflicts, in his
Unconscious. Many psychologists have concluded
from this that religion is an illusion of unconscious
phantasy and therefore irrational. But it is the conclusion that is irrational and fantastic. There is no
need to deny the facts. Properly understood they are

one of the main clues to the understanding of religion. The same psychologists tell us that the same childish attitudes largely determine the forms of our adult relations with one another. May it not then be the truth that what is reflected in our religion are the general forms and attitudes of our personal relations with one another? And if our religion is childish may that not simply reveal that our attitudes of mind and our ways of behavior, in our more intimate and direct relations with one another, are childish and fantastical? It would be easy to show that science itself arises in the same way as religion and is subject to the same explanation. There are still traces of childish phantasy about modern science, especially in those branches which are of recent growth; though it is true that science is on the whole much more sane and reasonable than it used to be. But it is not so very long since science too was the reflection of the child-life of phantasy. A few centuries ago—and that is only a moment in the history of humanity—science was the search for the elixir of life which would confer immortality on its discoverer, and the quest of the philosopher's stone which would transmute base metals into gold and confer unlimited wealth upon its possessor. Even Sir Isaac Newton cherished this latter hope, and a psychologist would have no difficulty in accounting for the way in which he threw his scientific researches overboard to become Master of the Royal Mint. But would anyone imagine that this proved that science was a mere projection of suppressed complexes, or conclude that science is irrational? The right conclusion is surely that until recently science was immature and undeveloped. It had not discovered itself or its true task. I submit, therefore, that the reflection of childish dreams in religion proves not that religion itself is irrational, but only that it is still immature and has not discovered its own meaning or its proper function. To this I must add that the spread of the conviction, in any community, that religion is a childish superstition is no evidence against the rationality of religion; but it is the strongest possible evidence that the personal relations of its members are irrational and that the community is in process of dissolution. For a community consists in the structure of personal relations between its members.

The other universal experience to which we must refer is the experience of being a member of a society. There is a close relation between the family and society; so close indeed that it has often been held that society is an enlargement of the primitive family group. There is a certain truth in this, if we are considering primitive society. But the history of social development, in which the two diverge more and more in their essential structure, is enough to show that from the beginning there is an essential difference between them. Family relations are essentially relations involving dependence. The family is based on the relation between parents and children, and on the need of children for care and protection. It is, therefore, held together by mutual affection. Society, on the other hand, is based upon relations of coöperation between adults for the provision of the necessities of life. It would not be true to say that either of these structures of relationships can be separated from the other. Coöperation leads or may lead to mutual affection, and the love-relations involve coöperation. But in the family the emphasis falls necessarily upon affection, while in society it falls upon coöperation and common interest. Affection can maintain the unity of the family even though coöperation is reduced to a minimum, while the community can be held together on a basis of material interest even though there is very little affection between its members. All human relations involve both the bond of affection and the bond of common interest in some degree. But the relations which constitute society subordinate affection to common interest, and rest the weight of their unity upon the need for economic coöperation and the division of labor. In the family coöperation has to be subordinated to the demands of natural affection.

We have seen how, in moments of stress, the bond of affection may be turned into opposition, and how the common life of coöperation may then preserve the relationship until affection is restored by forgiveness and reconciliation. In the case of society the reverse of this takes place. In times of stress, as for example when the society is threatened by attack from another society and its structure of coöperation for the supply of its needs is threatened with destruction, the society has to depend, for the preservation of its unity, upon the mutual affection of its members, that is to say, their emotional attachment and loyalty to one another as members of the same society. If that loyalty is not strong enough to preserve the unity until the normal working of its coöperative structure is restored, the society will perish. The more complicated the structure of coöperation in a society becomes, the more liable it is to break down. This means that it becomes more dependent upon the strength of the bonds of affection between its members. And the more extensive the society becomes the more difficult it becomes to create and sustain those bonds of common loyalty on which the possibility of effective coöperation depends. The development of society throughout history is fundamentally an increase in the numbers of people who become members of one society, that is to say, interdependent in coöperation for the supply of their needs. But this is possible only by the creation and maintenance of a bond of loyalty which unites an ever increasing number of people in loyalty to one another as members of the same human brotherhood. What is it, we have to ask, that enables the natural instincts of family affection to be extended farther and farther beyond the bounds of the natural family until it comes to embrace and hold together in a unity of affection masses of individuals who have never met one another face to face? What is it that in the long run has enabled us to conceive the idea of a universal

brotherhood of all mankind and to move toward it
through an extension of the network of coöperation
till today it comes near to making us all effectively
interdependent? This is not a theoretical question
merely. It is the practical problem that has faced human society from the beginning and which faces it
today.

History itself provides the answer. This is precisely the function of religion. In primitive society it
is quite clear that the function of religion is to create,
sustain, and express the emotional relationship which
unites the members of the primitive tribe. The close
connection of primitive religion with ancestor worship, the tendency for religious communities to trace
their descent to a common ancestor, the religious ceremonies which extend the relation of brotherhood to
people who are not natural brothers, often by the
symbolic mingling of their blood, and a thousand
other characteristics of primitive religion reveal very
clearly that its function is to extend the sentiments
which unite the members of the natural family beyond its natural limits. What is taking place is already the generalization of direct relationships of
natural affection. If we look to the development of religion in history, we find that the extension of this
bond of family affection to larger and larger groups
of people through the acceptance of a common faith
has been one of the controlling factors in the development of society. We are driven to the conclusion
that the function of religion is to increase the scope.

and the complexity of human coöperation by creating, sustaining, and expressing the union of persons in a spiritual family or a spiritual brotherhood. It should be noticed that the term "spiritual" here means merely "not related by blood." It does not mean "not material." Without such an extension of the sense of emotional unity beyond the natural field of its instinctive expression, the development of human society would have been impossible and the achievement of this is the work of religious reflection. We might express this shortly by saying that the task of religion is the maintenance and extension of human community. Religion is the only means by which this can be achieved.

We can now turn our attention to the reflective process itself by which religion is created. All reflective processes are processes of reason. We must beware of imagining that the only forms of rational activity are those of logical thinking. The reflective process by which a poem or a concerto is created is just as much a process of reason as any process by which a practical problem is solved, though it is not a process of reasoning. The process of reason which gives rise to religion is peculiar to religion, although it has relations to both scientific and artistic reflection. It is, indeed, a synthesis of both, and both are in fact derived from it. Religious reflection is the primary and the most comprehensive expression of human reason. What is basic to all the processes of reflection is that they are activities of imaginative construction with reference to a situation which is objectively given. Starting with experience they carry us beyond what is immediately given in experience. Yet it is in the propriety of their reference to experience that their rationality resides, however far they may pass beyond the boundaries of the immediately given. The mere activity of the imagination is in itself neither right nor wrong; its products are mere images, mere ideas, without reference to anything real. Imagination always transcends reality, but it is only rational when it is also immanent in reality. And reality is met with in the active processes of living, not in reflection. The world is not given in perception, since perception itself is only given in action. The philosopher's idea of perception is itself a process of reflection, or at the least it is the imaginary point at which action passes over into reflection. The *given* in our experience is the objective activity in which we relate ourselves, in the process of living our lives, to things other than ourselves. One of these activities, and the one which is the mainspring of human life, is the activity in which we relate ourselves to one another. It is this that is the *given* for religious reflection.

But since the activity of relation between persons is mutual, the primary aspect of religious reflection is also mutual. And since the primary activity of any form of reflection is the expression of the given fact, the primary activity of religious reflection is the mutual expression of the experience of mutual relation-

ship. If two people, or a group of people who share a
common life, have their experience of a common life
brought into the focus of their consciousness, their
mutual consciousness of community demands an expression for itself. Such an expression must be something that they do together to express their consciousness of a common life. It will therefore be at
once part of their common life, and yet the symbol
of it, and so transcending it. It must be a common activity set apart from all the other common activities
and so invested with a special significance. They may
dance together, or sing together, or simply eat together; but because they are doing such things to express the consciousness of their common life, the
dance will not be an ordinary dance but a sacred
dance; the song will be a sacred song, the meal a
sacred meal. These special activities of religious reflection will be symbols of their community, celebrations of their communion. On ordinary occasions they
do things together. On these special occasions they do
the same things together to express the fact that they
always are together in doing things; so that these
things become celebrations of their consciousness of
belonging to one another in a common life. Religious
ceremonial and ritual is then the primary reflective
activity of reason which starts from the ordinary experience of the mutuality of human life. The sacredness or sanctity which attaches to such symbolic com-
munal activities is nothing strange or paradoxical. It
is simply the fact that they are separated from all the

other common activities by the fact that they are undertaken to express the reflective recognition of their commonness.

But this celebration of community will not go very far by itself to explain the phenomena of religion. It is too positive, in that its possibility depends upon an experience of complete joy in harmonious coöperation, which must be very rare indeed, and which is in fact never continuous for long. It is doubtful indeed whether any reflective activity is possible which is not in some sense the product of contrast. It is when things go wrong that we stop to think them over. It is when community is broken, or in face of a threat to its satisfactory working, that we are brought to consciousness of it and of its importance to us. It is thus not merely the experience of a common life alone, but rather the experience of its precariousness that lies at the root of religious reflection. The element of fear for the unity of personal relationships seems always to be present in the reflective consciousness of them, and it heightens the consciousness of them. It is a commonplace that we never know how much other people mean to us till we have lost them. Indeed, the happier a friendship is the less conscious the friends are apt to be of it. But when relations are strained it is almost impossible to be unaware of them. It is the need to sustain and increase the sense of community which *requires* the activities which express it. Religious ceremonial, therefore, is never merely an expression of the consciousness of communion, it is also a means for sustaining it. It expresses at once the sense of community and the fear of its failure; and in so doing it strengthens and sustains the unity that it expresses. For whatever is brought into consciousness is by that very fact made an object of deliberate resolve. What was before merely something existing between the members of the group, becomes, through the activity of reflection, something *intended* by them all. It is this intention of relationship, supervening upon the mere fact of relationship, that constitutes the *differentia* of human or rational relationship, and makes it, in the widest sense, religious. It is not enough, for a rational being, that his relationship to the Other should be a fact. It must be also *intended*. It must be affirmed by his own will and choice. It must, moreover, be mutually affirmed and mutually chosen. As mere fact, at any stage, it is not enough; it must become more than mere fact; and the willing of it at once releases energies which transform it, even as fact. To put this formally, in affirming the community as intention the self negates it as fact. This synthesis of affirmation and negation is the structural characteristic of all religious reflection, and in its theoretical expression religion is, therefore, involved in paradoxes. To take but one instance from developed religion, it is impossible for the religious consciousness merely to affirm either the dependence of Man on God, or his independence of God. It must affirm both at once as complementary, because they are contradictory. It must affirm both the freedom of

Man and the omnipotence of God, both free choice and free grace, both responsibility and impotence. But what is expressed is a universal fact of human experience, in spite of the contradiction.

Religious reflection, then, makes the relationship of persons intentional, and so not merely actual but also possible. There are, that is to say, possibilities in it which did not exist before. It might be more intimate, more harmonious, more extensive, more effective as well as more fully realized in reflective consciousness by the persons united in it. The immediate effect of the consciousness of community is thus to reveal to reflection the imperfection of the actual community and the possibility of its perfecting. As in any other field, the result of reflection is to enlarge the scope of the actual, which is always the present, to include the past and the future. The intentionality which is inseparable from this reflection is realized as a motive for deliberately continuing the relationship into the future and making its future better than its past. We must consider this reference to the future in its two main aspects. It results in the direction of conscious effort to the conservation of relationships already actual. It also results in the effort to develop actual relationships and so to realize their possibilities.

The primary task which faces religious reflection in its conservative aspect is the liability of relations to be broken. This breaking of relationships is possible both at the level of actuality and at the level of intentionality. The fact of death involves the breaking of relationships at the level of actuality. For this reason a great deal of primitive religion has been concerned to secure the survival of personality in spite of death, and has devised all sorts of religious ceremonies to achieve this or at least to symbolize it. But such activity must always remain problematical, since no proof of its effectiveness is possible, and it is always the *effective* continuation of relationship that is the demand. But the problem of death has a quite immediate and direct importance for religious reflection, since one very important aspect of the conservation of personal relationships is the problem of the conservation of the communities of relationship in spite of the death of their members. The family is intentionally preserved from generation to generation and the unity of its later members is directly dependent upon its continuity with the relationships of individuals who are now dead. This enables us to understand why and in what sense religion has always been profoundly exercised about the preservation of family life, and equally, though not so intensively, with the preservation of the continuity of the particular society whose religion it is. In both cases it is the fear of the actual destruction of the personal relationships already established that is the determining factor.

But it is at the level of intentionality that the conservative function of religious reflection is most crea-

tive, because it is in this field that there is the widest
scope for its effective action. A relationship may remain actual as the sharing of a common life and yet
be broken in consciousness by a clash of wills. The intention to maintain a common life may remain,
though the individuals concerned find themselves out
of touch and out of sympathy with one another or
even actually hostile. Or the intention to maintain the
common life may disappear and be replaced by the
desire to break it, while the common life is maintained
by necessities from which there is no escape or appears to be none. In this case the main task of reflection is to restore the mutual intentionality of the
relationship. Now this depends, in the last analysis,
upon a change in the wills of the individuals between
whom conscious mutuality has been broken. It cannot
be done for them by any outside agency, though a
mediator between them may be essential. Nor can it
be achieved by any of them separately. Reconciliation must be mutual or it cannot take place. The
problem of religion is, therefore, how this mutual
reconciliation can be brought about. This introduces
at once the problem of sin, for the conception of sin
is originally the conception of that wrong which
breaks fellowship between persons. Whatever brings
two persons into contradiction or opposition with one
another is sin. It is, therefore, that which requires
forgiveness if its consequences—the alienation which
it produces—are to be abolished and reconciliation

achieved. In this aspect of its task, religion becomes the search for the means of overcoming sin and achieving reconciliation.

One aspect of this is of special importance. If a relation between two persons is broken in this way, the reflective activity which is concerned with its restoration ceases to be mutual. The individuals become separated and isolated in their conscious life. Each of them feels wronged by the other. The natural tendency of each in reflection is, therefore, to accuse the other, to fix the blame for the break upon the other, and so to increase his own isolation and to thwart tendencies to reconciliation. In that state of alienation, reconciliation is impossible and will remain impossible unless it is altered. The paradox of the situation is that the state of consciousness which needs the reconciliation makes the reconciliation impossible. What is required is repentance, that the state of consciousness should be radically altered. But how can a state of consciousness alter itself in opposition to its own nature. That is the source of the dilemma which expresses itself in the religious paradox that man is helpless to save himself from sin and yet that his salvation can only come about through his own free action. How can two isolated individuals act mutually? How can the isolation be overcome except by a mutual act? This problem must have a solution, because the thing happens again and again in our experience. Religion seeks to understand and to make available the means for its universal solution.

The conservative activity of religious reflection is, however, only its negative aspect. Its positive aspect is the realization of the possibilities of relationships. This, in turn, has two aspects. There is the possibility of increasing the range of community so that it includes a larger number of persons. There is also the possibility of increasing the depth and intensity of communion. The element of possibility which is inherent in religious reflection has thus both a quantitative and a qualitative side. These are not strictly separable, since there is a direct relationship between the intensity of the conscious community and the numbers of persons that it can unify. We may, however, consider them separately.

There is a tendency in coöperation to expand the number of persons included in a coöperative group. Other things being equal, the larger the group is, the more effective and productive coöperation becomes. The mere consciousness of needs which can only be met through the coöperation of a larger group, itself creates the desire for a wider community of coöperation. This will lead to an actual coöperation which is motived purely by its profitableness to the persons concerned, but which includes no intention of personal relation. In such cases we find that a society of actual relationship is set up, but it is not supported by any consciousness of community. Such a society can remain actual so long as it is immediately beneficial; so long, that is to say, as it is not subjected to a stress which endangers it. But the moment such a stress appears, it will necessarily break down, unless it can be sustained by a personal loyalty. Such a society is, therefore, precarious and superficial, while the relations which constitute it are unconscious. If these relations are brought to consciousness, they must either be affirmed as personal relations or repudiated. In either case the situation is profoundly altered. It is no longer a question of the existence or nonexistence of coöperation, but of the acceptance or refusal of community. Community refused means hatred, opposition and war. This is an aspect of the question which I need not elaborate. It is illustrated on a world-wide scale in the international situation in which we live. In our time the consciousness of community is, at its widest effective limit, national. But the last century saw the creation, which was unintentional, of a network of economic coöperation which crossed national boundaries and became almost worldwide. Quite recently that network of human relationship had to meet a stress that tended to destroy it. The effect of this world-wide economic catastrophe has been to bring the relations which constituted it to consciousness. The result is that now we must either affirm these relationships on the intentional plane and so create a world-wide community, or we must repudiate them. If we do repudiate them, we must restrict coöperation once more within the limits of the existing communities, while remaining conscious of the possibility which we are refusing. In that case, the refusal becomes an act of hostility and leads inevitably in the direction of active hostility and war.

The creation of such an extended community is the task of religion, since it is the task of creating the intention of personal relationship between masses of people in whom the intention does not exist. The reflective activity which is involved in this extension of community is of the same type as that involved in the conservative function. It is only its direction which is different. It has to preserve and deepen the existing sense of community, while extending it, and in that extension the same problems recur. But in this case the primary problem is that of overcoming hostility and isolation and of achieving the reconciliation, while at each stage of the achievement what has been achieved must be maintained, if there is to be further advance toward a complete solution.

The other aspect of the positive function of religious reflection is to realize intentionally the qualitative possibilities of personal relationships. This is characteristic of the development of all reflective life. In science, for example, development has the same two aspects. It consists in bringing wider and wider ranges of fact within the scope of scientific unification. But it also consists in a continuous improvement in the quality of our understanding of the same facts. In science this is achieved by a double process in which the reflection upon experience already achieved is succeeded by the intentional achievement of new experience based upon the result of the reflection. It is the same in religion. The consciousness of relationship makes the relationship intentional. The intention expresses itself in the effort to realize the relationship in new ways and to find new expressions for it. And these new experiences of relationship become in turn the objects of reflection. In this way the meaning and significance of personal relations is gradually disclosed to reflection. The ways in which the intention of love can be mutually realized and manifested are made operative in a wider range of activities. In principle religion differs here from science only in the fact, which we have already noticed, that its reflective and practical aspects are more intimately interwoven.

Such, it seems to me, is the natural structure of the self in its religious reflection. These are the activities of its reflection upon the nexus of personal relationship in which it is involved, and the practical activities which give effect to the results of this reflection. They are its ways of dealing with its own inherent mutuality. I have purposely refrained from giving prominence to that aspect of religious reflection which is concerned with understanding and thought, or with the mutuality of understanding and thought, which is speech. In religion thought and understanding, though they play an important part, are strictly subordinate. They are subordinate because the part played by thought and speech in the mutual relations of individuals, though important, is subordinate.

40984

Even our direct knowledge of one another is not primarily the result of reflective thought and its expression, though indirectly this function of reflection plays an important part. I mean in particular that people do not get to know one another by discussing their relation to one another, but by discussing other things. The primary expressions of reflective mutuality are symbolic actions, and their expression in speech tends primarily to be symbolic, metaphorical, or mythical. But there is one idea which is inseparable from religious reflection after it has reached a. very primitive stage of development to which I must refer in closing this chapter. It is the idea of God. Any form of reflection, since it raises actual experience to the level of intentionality, carries the self beyond the limits of the actual given. As a result it involves the universalizing of the actual experience which is the object of reflection. Reflection reveals the universal in the particular. Now if the object of reflection is the relation of the self to another self, the universal which is so revealed must be universal personality. On the other hand, it cannot be a universal in the ordinary logical sense, which is that of a common essence expressed in each of a number of particulars. That is only possible when the self is the observer of a world which does not include him as part of the object of reflection. In religion it is the mutuality between the self and another self which is the object of reflection. The universal, therefore, must be a universal person to whom the self stands in universal relation. The idea of God as the universal Other is, therefore, inherent in the act of religious reflection. It is given in the act of reflection itself, which starts from the actual fact of personal relationships. The universal cannot be denied, since to deny it would be to deny the act of reflection, while it is only through the act of reflection that the denial is possible. The existence of God cannot, therefore, be rationally denied, since it cannot be denied without self-contradiction. And since, as we have seen, religious reflection is the primary form of reflection from which scientific and artistic reflection are derived and in which they are contained, God is the primary correlate of human rationality. Moreover, because religious reflection is not primarily expressed in thought but in action, God is not primarily apprehended as an idea, but in life which is centered in the intention of mutuality, as that infinite personality in which our finite human relationships have their ground and their being.

III

THE REFERENCE OF RELIGIOUS IDEAS

THE self in religious activity is the self in reflective activity in the religious field, that is to say, in the field of personal relationships. As we have seen, the effect of this is to raise the life of personal relationship to the intentional level, and so to universalize it. Now, when any activity becomes conscious, deliberate, or intentional, it is performed at a level where there is the possibility of error. All reflective activity is characterized by the fact that it can be performed rightly or wrongly. Since religion is a reflective activity, religion itself can be either good or bad. Religious activity, just because it is reflective, is capable of being rightly or wrongly directed. Any treatment of religion which ignores the distinction between truth and error in religion must, therefore, be mistaken or at least incomplete. It seems to me that, in the main, current accounts of religious experience, whether they are critical or enthusiastic, are vitiated by their failure to recognize this. They treat religion as something which simply exists, and inquire whether it is good that it should exist or not. They are either in favor of religion or against it. If this attitude is adopted, it is impossible to raise the really essential question of distinguishing between religious activities which are right, and religious activities which are wrong, between religious assertions which are true and religious assertions which are false, between religious emotions which are rational and religious emotions which are sentimental or vicious. It is no use setting out to justify religion as a whole, since a glance at the history of religion shows that a great deal of it has been unjustifiable and even grossly immoral. Neither is it possible to justify religious belief in general, since there have been and still are religious beliefs which are palpably nonsense, and because there are obvious contradictions between the beliefs held by different religious people, even within the limits of contemporary Christianity itself. It is only what is valid in religion that can be justified, and it can only be justified by distinguishing it from what is not valid and rejecting that as spurious. That which makes truth possible makes error possible, and that which makes good possible also makes evil possible. No reflective activity can be justified except in so far as it achieves truth and validity, and escapes error and falsity.

We are faced, therefore, with the necessity of raising the question of the distinction between rightness and wrongness in religious reflection. It is this question which I wish to discuss as the problem of the reference of religious ideas. This is, indeed, a one-sided approach to the question, since religion is not primarily a matter of ideas, for reasons which we have already discussed. But it is easier and more familiar to examine this aspect of the general question, because, though it is a subordinate one, it illustrates more simply than any other the meaning of the problem in its whole complexity. But it will be as well to guard against misunderstanding by indicating at once the general relation that holds between religious ideas and religious activity in its more primary character.

The mutuality of human beings is the central fact of human experience. For this reason all human activities have a bearing upon the community of persons and affect its character. For the same reason religious activity includes scientific and artistic activity. Community between any two persons leads each to consider his private activities in relation to the other; to labor, that is to say, for the benefit of the other. Equally it involves each in the artistic activity of appreciating and enjoying the other. This is a way of saying that the field of science and the field of art are included in the religious sphere. They are taken up out of their individuality into the mutuality of personal relationships, and so united in the only way in which they can be united. Their conscious forms include one another in the same fashion. The religious intention includes the scientific and the artistic. The intention of religion, when it has fully unfolded itself in consciousness, is the redemption of the world, the achieving of a universal reconciliation between persons. This must include the achievement of universal coöperation for the satisfaction of individual needs and a universal appreciation of all men by all men. These two components of the religious intention become respectively, when cut loose in consciousness from the idea of community, the intentions of science and of art. Science and art, therefore, live within religion and are derived from it by a concentration upon one or other of its two components. This is only a reflective way of stating the fact that science and art are made possible by the existence of human communities.

This dissociation of the two components of the religious consciousness shows itself in the fact that science concentrates on intellectual reflection while art concentrates on emotional reflection, and both, in order to do so, must withdraw from practical activity. Religion, however, because it contains these two components in its unity, and so constitutes the full reflective activity of the self, unifies intellectual and emotional activity and does not require to withdraw from practical life. It merely raises it as a whole to the level of intentionality. This is the reason why, as we have seen, the primary religious expression is a common action done to express the community of all actions in the common life. Specific religious activities are at once parts of the common life and expressions of the unity of all the activities of the society in a common life. But the *development* of religious reflection demands a withdrawal from practical activity, in order to permit of the concentration of reflection upon one or other of the two components —the intellectual or the emotional. Thus we find that there is always a rhythm of withdrawal and return in the religious life—withdrawal into individual solitariness, which expresses the need for thought and contemplation; and return to the life of community with the intention of personal relationship intensified and developed. For the same reason the moment of solitariness takes two forms, an emotional form and an intellectual one. The former corresponds to art, the latter to science. But they differ from science and art in that they are carried on in the full consciousness of mutuality. They are seen in reflection as part of the religious life and not as separate and independent activities of the individual. The emotional or artistic reflection within religious reflection, therefore, issues in mysticism or solitary religious contemplation. The scientific or intellectual gives rise to religious thought, that is to say, to philosophy or theology. For philosophy and theology are ultimately one and the same form of reflection. Their difference is accidental in principle and merely indicates that one or the other, or both, are in error. Of these two components of the moment of withdrawal in religious reflection, the emotional or contemplative lies nearer to the moment of primary expression in the act of communion. This is because emotion lies nearer to action than intellect, since it contains the motive forces of action. Before an intellectual conclusion can become effective in action, an emotional motive must be provided which the intellect itself does not contain. But an emotional reflection can determine action directly, and indeed will do so if it is not checked by fear. Thus in religion it is the field of thought, doctrine, and theology—the field of intellectual understanding—that lies furthest from the immediate experience which gives rise to reflection.

The importance of this lies in the nature of the relation between religious thought and practical activity. It is the reverse of the relation between scientific thought and practical activity. The practical function of scientific reflection is to enable us to use the material available in the world more effectively for the achievement of our purposes. The understanding of things is in this case preliminary to the possibility of using them. Its effect is to provide a plan of action which can then be followed. But in religion, thought is not concerned with the formation of plans. The function of religious reflection is to strengthen and develop the intention of mutuality. It is a commonplace that personal capacity cannot be increased or developed by acting according to a plan, but only by exercising it in its natural field. "Which of you, by taking thought," said Jesus, "can add a cubit to his stature?" In religion intellectual expression does not precede but follows the actual experience of practical activity. Religious doctrines, like philosophical doctrines, are the expression of an experience which is already achieved. They are not rules for achieving things which could not otherwise be achieved. Their reference to action is indirect. They raise the level of reflective consciousness and so increase the range of intention. Understanding in the religious field enables us to know what we are doing and so to do it better. In the scientific field understanding enables us to do something that we wanted to do but were unable to do without it. Scientific understanding is concerned with the tactics of life, religious understanding with its essence.

The importance of this for our purpose is the corollary that the most serious falsification of religious reflection does not lie in errors of intellectual belief. In science the truth or falsity of its assertions is the whole issue, because if they are not true they defeat our intention in action. They make the action altogether unsuccessful. In religion such mistaken beliefs are important, but they do not make religious activity impossible. If people want to talk to one another at a distance, they can only do so by inventing the telephone, and they can only invent the telephone by a true scientific understanding. But though no doubt an understanding of human nature may help people to get on together better, it does not necessarily do so, and a purely fictitious understanding of human nature does not prevent people from living together in harmony. The falsification of religion that matters most, even in the sphere of religious thought, is not the ultimate truth or falsity of beliefs, but the falsification of the reference of these beliefs to experience.

All reflective activities which involve a withdrawal from action are subjective, since they involve the ab-

straction of reflection from the primary activities of
life. Yet they are still parts of life and fall within its
primary nature. They are abstracted within the activity of living, not abstracted from it. Such activities are subjective because they are carried on within
the self and are not activities in which the self enters
into relation with other things or other selves. In all
our activities there is, of course, a subjective element.
But it is inseparably bound up with the practical op-
erations of our bodies upon other bodies. We are used
to refer to this subjective element in our experience
as our mind or our consciousness. A subjective activity is an activity in which our consciousness is reflected back upon itself and so becomes the center of
interest and effort. The intention of our activity is, in
such reflection, the development of our consciousness,
so that the increase and development of consciousness
becomes an end in itself.

The primary subjective activity is the activity of
imagination. It consists in the formation and development of images in the mind. When carried on for its
own sake it is, as it were, a kind of intentional dreaming which has no specific purpose and which, therefore, can, in itself, be performed neither rightly nor
wrongly. A subjective process, that is to say, so far
as it is self-contained, cannot be right or wrong and
cannot involve truth or falsity. It is strictly meaningless and purposeless. But since it can only exist
within a life that is objective, since it can only take
place in a self which lives in relation to other things

and other selves, it always must have a relation to
reality. Even our dreams in sleep have a relation to
our waking experience, although in dreaming we are
not conscious of this relation. But when we are conscious of the relation between our subjective activities and our objective experience, then the relation of
the two becomes intentional. We refer our images to
things. We refer our ideas to reality. Whenever a
subjective activity is so referred to the objective
world within which it is a subjective element, it is
either rightly or wrongly referred and is, therefore,
capable of being true or false. For our present purpose we need not raise the interesting question
whether ideas and thoughts are images or not. They
are certainly elements in the subjective aspect of our
experience and the processes of thought which are
concerned with ideas are processes in consciousness,
that is to say, subjective processes. What is important for our purpose is to note that the possibility of
rightness and wrongness or of truth and falsity in
our subjective activity, is bound up with the reference to objective experience; and since objective experience is practical experience—for it is only in
practical experience that we enter into relations with
objects—the possibility of subjective activities being
right or wrong and having meaning in them is bound
up with their reference to practical activity.

The question of truth and falsity in religion is
therefore fundamentally a question of the reference
of the subjective activities of the self in religion to

objective reality. Until we know what an idea refers
to, or what a thought is about, we cannot say whether
it is true or false. We must be conscious of its relation to something that is not an idea or a thought.
But there is a difficulty about this which is the result
of the religious character of experience. The mutuality of human life is not annulled by the withdrawal
of the individual into the solitariness of his own sub-
jectivity, and this shows itself in the fact that his
ideas may refer not directly to objects but to the
ideas and thoughts of other selves. If this reference is
intentional the ideas can be true or false in a qualified sense. I may say rightly that a dragon is a
winged serpent in spite of the fact that there are no
dragons. I may say that Sir John Falstaff was a very
fat, drunken English knight. I may even say that
Cleopatra was very beautiful and fascinating and be
contradicted by a historian. I shall then say that I
was referring to Shakespeare's Cleopatra, and that
she *was* very fascinating and beautiful, and if that
was a mistake it was Shakespeare's mistake and not
mine. That is to say, the imagination can create
worlds which are fictitious, either unconsciously, as in
popular mythology, or deliberately, as the artist or
dramatist does. And because these fictitious worlds
of the imagination can be shared by people, the ideas
of any one of them can be true or false in reference
to a world of mutual fiction. On the other hand, these
fictitious worlds always have some reference to the
real world of practical experience, or they could not

even be shared. And they may have an intentional reference even though it is symbolic. In the latter case, a person who does not understand the symbolism will be unable to grasp the meaning or reference that is intended, and for him the world of reference will be purely fictitious, imaginary, and meaningless.

But that is not the whole story. Both in the history of society and in the life history of an individual a set of ideas which once had a conscious and significant relation to objective experience may lose it. Many ancient myths certainly once had a conscious and significant reference to the everyday experience of common life. They were true in the sense that the people who believed them recognized them as referring quite properly to their own direct experience. But they have become for us mere fairy tales or pure fiction with only an æsthetic interest. Similarly in the life of an individual, ideas, particularly symbolic ideas, which once had a conscious significance in relation to his experience, may, with the lapse of time and change of circumstance, lose their meaning because their reference has been forgotten. He can remember that they were once significant for him, but he cannot remember why or even imagine how they could have been. The reference to reality has been obliterated and lost.

All this has a very direct bearing upon the question of truth in religion. Before that question can be properly asked and investigated we must know how religion refers, in its subjective activities, to reality.

The facts that we have just considered show that this is not the simple and straightforward question that it might seem at first sight. The reference of an idea to experience is not simply a fact which exists whether anyone is conscious of it or not. It is a matter of intention. But neither is it true that it is *merely* a matter of intention, because the intentional reference of an idea does not make it true. It merely makes it capable of being either true or false. Without an intentional reference to common experience, religious reflection is a meaningless play of imagination. With it, it is significant but not necessarily true. There are at least four possibilities. Religious ideas may be entertained without being referred to reality. They may be referred to reality wrongly. They may be referred to reality rightly. Or, lastly, they may be referred by some people and not by others, at one time and not at another time, rightly by some people and wrongly by others, or rightly at one time and wrongly at another.

One thing, however, we may assert at once. Religious ideas always have a *potential* reference to reality. To deny this would be to say that it was possible to have a religion which was not meant to have any reality and which did not claim to have any serious significance. That, I think, we may rule out without further argument. If anyone were to maintain that he was religious but that his religion was a mere play of fancy which he did not take seriously, we should know at once that he was merely playing with words. Whether religion has real significance or not, it is meant to have a significance and believed to have a significance or it is not religion at all. This might seem to rule out our first alternative. But it does not. It only alters its character. It is still possible for people to entertain religious ideas and engage in religious practices without referring them to the reality of common experience. What is impossible is that they should be unaware that they involve a reference. The failure to refer them is, then, a refusal to refer them to reality which must be compensated by a substitute reference.

It is this point in particular which I wish to emphasize. The necessity of referring religion to the reality of common experience and so relating it to the reality of actual life can be avoided by referring it away from the world of common experience to another world which is not experienced but only imagined. Thus, there arises in religion the idea of a world which is supernatural, and its function is to allow religious reflection to be carried on without any explicit reference to the facts of experience, and so without the intention of a return to practical life in terms of the religious reflection. It is in this way that religious reflection can be made an end in itself and the essential unity of reflection and action which characterizes the field of religion can be broken. When this is done religious reflection becomes unreal. This other world must, of course, be thought and felt to be real. Otherwise the reference could not be made. The imaginary world must be imagined as real. But it has to be a world which is imagined to be at once real and beyond the possibility of direct experience, for it must be a world in which we are not called upon to act in practical life.

The primary falsification of religious reflection is thus the dissociation of its subjective activities from their embodiment in the activities of empirical life. It is the dissociation of the moment of withdrawal in the rhythm of religious life from the moment of return. We must consider for a moment some of the more important consequences of this dissociation. The first is that it involves a dualism in consciousness which creates two worlds instead of one. One of these is the world which is experienced in practical activity, the other a world which is only experienced in reflection. Both of these worlds are asserted to be real, though in different senses. But this dual reality is a constant problem, since they cannot both be real for the self at the same time. In its religious reflection one of the two worlds becomes the focus of reference and, therefore, becomes real; while the other correspondingly becomes shadowy and unreal. When the same self returns to practical life the reverse happens. The natural world becomes the focus of reference and the supernatural world becomes correspondingly unreal and unsubstantial. It is precisely the impossibility of taking both as real at once that is the unconscious motive of the falsification, because it is precisely this that maintains the dissociation. If the two worlds of

reference were really taken as real in the same sense
and at the same time, they would no longer be two
worlds but one and the same. It is one thing to realize
that the world in which we live is wider and deeper
than we know, and that there may be whole reaches of
it and aspects of it which are hidden from our normal
consciousness. It is quite another thing to hold that
there is another world which is not this world at all.
It is one thing to say that religion is about the other
world. It is a very different thing to say that it is
about an aspect of this world to which we are usually
blind. The first statement is a falsification of religion
which makes it unreal. The second is the truth of real
religion. We have only to imagine what would be the
effect upon science if we were to hold that scientific
statements were statements about a world of electrons
and electrical forces which was a different world from
the world in which we live here and now, instead of
holding that they are a discovery of facts about the
world in which we now live, which can only be known
through scientific reflection and research. If we
thought this, science would no longer have any bearing upon practical life, and its essential nature would
be falsified. It is interesting to notice that some scientists in our own day have come very near to saying
this about science. Professor Eddington, for example,
has said that science is not really talking about the
physical world at all but only about pointer readings
and measurements.

As a result of this primary dissociation, religion

becomes a private matter for the individual. It is no longer, that is to say, essentially a matter of real mutuality, but a relation of the individual in reflection to his own ideals and aspirations. Consequently, it no longer carries the intention of a return to an increasing range and intensity of common life. Religion becomes "what an individual does with his solitariness," to use a phrase to which Professor Whitehead has given currency. But this means that when the individual does return to the practical life of mutual relationship he returns to it at the nonreflective, unintentional level, and the function of religion in relation to practical mutuality is frustrated. Religion, in this way, ceases to function in relation to normal life. The same holds true of a society whose religion has become "other-wordly." It is dissociated from the mutual coöperation of the common life. The reference from one to the other is no longer recognized. The real life of the society is then a secular life, and its intentional basis is deprived of the support of the religious consciousness and becomes a mere coöperation undirected by the intention of fellowship. In that case, any threat to its structure leaves the society unable to sustain the system of coöperation through the sense of brotherhood in adversity. Its religion has become socially ineffective and functionless.

This statement, however, requires a qualification. It is only at the level of intention or explicit consciousness that the dissociation can take place. A religion which refers its ideas to another world does not thereby destroy their actual reference to this world. To put it in psychological terms which are familiar, the reference remains unconscious. Its ideas, though they are referred in explicit consciousness to the other world, function in the individual or the society as unconscious symbols of the existing community. Now, it is characteristic of unconscious symbols that they remain undeveloped. They refer, that is to say, not to the existing state of social life but to a state of social life to which they were originally consciously referred at the time of their formation. A child whose religious ideas and attitudes are formed in the family circle, and whose later development dissociates his religious reflection from his normal activities, will retain a childish conception of the other world. His religion will be a generalization of his experience as a child in the family circle, because this was the practical experience to which it was consciously referred in his past life. The religion of a society which has become dissociated from the secular relationships of its members will retain an unconscious reference to the secular life of the community as it was at the time when the dissociation set in. For this reason a dissociated religion works as a powerful conservative agency. Indeed, its effect is to attach to the past a feeling of sacredness which the present has lost, and to produce a craving for a return to more primitive conditions of life. In a progressive society this must have a cumulative effect. The further its organization of common life develops, the greater becomes the difference between its contemporary structure and the original structure to which its religious ideas properly refer. The religion, therefore, has progressively less potentiality of reference to the contemporary reality of common life. Now the forms of community which change most slowly are precisely those forms which were earliest established in human development, and the family, which is the earliest of all, is the most persistent. We have seen that the social function of religion is the extension of the family unity of affection to wider and wider groups. We can now see that the dissociation of religion through the reference to another world produces, when accompanied by a development of secular society, precisely opposite results. For the reference, unconscious though it remains, is gradually restricted, even in its conservative function, to a narrowing range, which converges upon the family. It can only refer to those elements in the social structure which have resisted most successfully the general change in the structure of social relationships. The falsification of religion, precisely because it involves a mere conservation of existing forms, actually works toward the disintegration of the community. A society with a dissociated religion, while becoming wider in its system of cooperation, becomes progressively less and less of a community. The range and intensity of community is progressively decreased. There comes a point at which the society, in order to sustain the system of

coöperation in times of stress, is driven to attack its
religion and so to hasten its own dissolution.

The dualism which arises from the reference of religious ideas away from the empirical experience of
common life expresses itself in a multitude of forms
with which we are, unhappily, only too familiar. It
appears as the disjunction between secular and sacred, between human and divine, between the natural
and the supernatural, between body and soul; or,
with a somewhat different intonation, between reason
and emotion, between matter and mind, between indi-
vidualism and socialism. A dissociation which has its
roots in the religious field must spread through every
part of individual and social life and lead slowly but
surely to complete disintegration. What God has
joined man puts asunder at his peril. But to trace its
ramifications would carry us too far afield. Instead, I
shall leave the analysis at the point the argument has
reached, and present, in as simple a form as I can
compass, the view of religion to which it points.

We belong to the order of Nature, but if that were
the whole truth, we should not be human beings. Our
humanity consists in the fact that we *know* that we
are part of the order of Nature, and live in that
knowledge. In this we transcend the natural order
while remaining immanent in it. The spiritual world
to which, by our transcendence of the natural order,
we belong is not another world, but the natural world
known and intended. We live in the natural world in

good truth; but we know it and know that we are living in it. Because of this knowledge our actions, so far as they are human, are intentional; and our intentions, directed upon the natural world that our knowledge reveals, transform it and all that it contains. It is no longer a world of fact, but a world of possibility; no longer an existing present, but a world with a future. So we have our being in a spiritual world which is the natural world of existence raised to a higher power by our capacity for reflection and the intentionality which reflection confers upon our activities. It is *this* world which is the real world; not the world of fact but the world of significance; the world of fact become possibility, become existence with a meaning, a future, and a destiny. For a fact known is no longer merely a fact. It is a possibility of transformation.

The focus of all human experience is to be found in our relations to one another. Our life is a shared life, our experience a common experience. There is one world for us all, and we all know it. We do not live in private worlds of our own. We are parts of the personal world, which is simply the natural world penetrated and transformed by personal purposes. As parts of this world we are members one of another; we belong together in community. This also is a thing that we all know. It is a matter of empirical and universal experience. And it is only in relation to this fact that anything in the world can be properly known. Forget it, and the world ceases to be a personal world and sinks to the level of mere brute fact, without meaning or significance, without room for any intention or any possibility. Such a world is quite unreal, because it is no longer the world in which we live. Remember that fact and at once we are back again in the real world with the mutuality of our common life at its heart.

This real world which we know and share, in which we love and hate, achieve and are frustrated, live and die, is the world of religion. This is the primary point which I am concerned to maintain. Religion is firmly rooted in our universal, common experience. It arises from our ordinary experience of living in the world in relation with other people and to that experience it refers. My second assertion is that, so soon as this fact of our relationship to others is brought to focus in our reflective consciousness, religion is born. The only way to avoid religion is to avoid the consciousness that we are members of the community. The only way to reject religion is to reject, deny, or ignore our direct relationship to one another. But since this relationship is a fact from which there can be no escape, to deny it is merely to refuse to face the facts. However tightly we shut our eyes, it makes no difference to the fact of our interdependence. Religion is simply the recognition of this fact and of its importance, and true religion is its acceptance with all its implications. The religious man in the only true sense is the man for whose life this fact has been recognized as the fact of primary significance in all life and in whom it has become not merely a fact but an intention. The mainspring of his activity is the intention to maintain, extend, and perfect the interdependence of persons in community.

With intention there appears a transcendence of the natural order of fact. The contrast between the actual and the possible emerges and life becomes the deliberate effort to realize the possibilities of the world as it is. But this effort introduces into life a polarity between action and reflection. What is possible must be imagined before it can be achieved. The rhythm of human life swings to and fro between the withdrawal from action into reflection which is its negative phase, and the return from reflection to action which is its positive phase. In religion, the positive phase is the set of activities in which conscious community is expressed, enlarged, deepened, and achieved. The negative phase is the reflection in which the possibilities of community are discovered in thought, imagination, and symbol. The two poles have significance only in relation to one another, and, therefore, the reality of religion consists in their living union; and religion is real only in the full rhythm which moves from one to the other and back again. But religious reflection has a peculiarity which arises from the fact that the religious experience is an experience of mutuality, and reflection cannot, in most of its aspects, be mutual. Its reflective phase must be individual and solitary even though individuals may meet together to engage in it. In this solitariness of religious reflection, since it is a withdrawal from active coöperation into imagination, love, which is the motive force of mutual activity, becomes a sentiment, and the community to which it is directed becomes an idea. Unless the sentiment and the idea are sustained by the intention to return to the real world of coöperative action to which they refer, they cease to be real. The sentiment becomes sentimentality, the idea becomes mere imagination. Their reality lies beyond them. The justification and the validity of religious reflection lie only in the intention to develop our feeling and our understanding of mutuality beyond the point at which it is actually developed in practical coöperation, in order that we may thereby return to the world of practical mutuality with an enhanced capacity for harmonious coöperation and a strengthened and enlightened intention of achieving it.

In the third place, it is characteristic of religion that in reflection it tends to divide into two phases, an emotional and an intellectual one. The reason is that the unity of thought and emotion can only be properly achieved in action. What holds the two together in religious reflection is only the intention to return to the activities of practical coöperation. If this intention is broken we have two unrelated forms of religious reflection, the mystical and the theological or philosophical. Now, either of these can be referred to reality separately, in which case the reference will be to an aspect of practical activity. Intellectual reflection will refer to that aspect of practical life in which the world is a means for the achievement of our ends. When this side of reflection is separated from its unity with the other in religious reflection, it ceases to be religious and becomes scientific. When the other is so separated and separately referred, it becomes artistic. It is in this way that art and science arise from religion, and it is only in religion that they can be unified. This sets up an opposition in the life of society between its scientific and its artistic aspects. Technical progress and the development of that fineness or refinement in living which we call culture find themselves in opposition and pull the society in different directions at once. In a society which has lost the religious intention, culture and technology find themselves necessarily at war.

Lastly, there is a simple reason for the tendency to dissociate the reflective aspect of religion from its practical aspect, and so to turn religion into sentimentality and illusion. The achievement of satisfactory mutual relationships in real life is not merely the primary task which life sets us, it is also the hardest and the one from which we most easily recoil. Reflection reveals not merely a world of possibility but a world of fear, and of all things in the world we fear one another most. Anyone who has made the attempt to create a common life of intimate relationships with another person—and everyone who has been married has made the attempt—must know just how difficult it is, and how natural it is to give up the task and be content in practice with the achievement of a reason-

ably satisfactory compromise which falls far short of
the intention with which the effort began. The dreams
of a complete and perfect intimacy over the whole
range of a life completely shared remain. But the intention to realize them in practice is weakened and
disappears. The task, we feel, is beyond us. It is
enough, and something to be proud of, if we can sustain such a unity as we have achieved without serious
breakdown. The dissociation of religious reflection
from the effort to achieve the possibility that it reveals is simply this problem universalized. In its full
unfolding, religious reflection reveals the possibility
of a universal community of mankind, of a perfectly
harmonious coöperation of all men irrespective of differences, in a spirit of universal brotherhood. Is it
any matter for surprise that a religious community,
like the Christian Church, which set out to achieve
the brotherhood of mankind in active and universal
coöperation, should be staggered by the tragic im-
mensity of the task set for it and become content with
the little that it has achieved? Nevertheless, this res-
ignation is failure and results in the falsification and
decline of religion. For religion then becomes a matter of sentiment and idea which there is no longer any
effective intention of carrying into operation in the
actuality of economic interdependence.